Hits and Missives

poems by

Carol H. Jewell

Clare Songbirds Publishing House Chapbook Series
ISBN 978-1-947653-10-8
Clare Songbirds Publishing House
Hits & Missives © 2017 Carol H. Jewell

Printed in the United States of America
FIRST EDITION

Clare Songbirds Publishing House Mission Statement:
Clare Songbirds Publishing House was established to provide
a print forum for the creation of limited edition, fine art from
poets and writers, both established and emerging. We strive to
reignite and continue a tradition of quality, accessible literary
arts to the national and international community of writers, and
readers. Chapbook manuscripts and art quality poetry
broadsides are carefully chosen for their ability to propel the
expansion of art and ideas in literary form. We provide an
accessible way to promote the art of words in order to resonate
with, and impact, readers not yet familiar with the siren song of
poets and writers. Clare Songbirds Publishing House espouses
a singular cultural development where poetry creates
community and becomes commonplace in public places.

Clare Songbirds Publishing House
140 Cottage Street
Auburn, New York 13021

Contents

Acknowledgements

"Cento Pantoum #1" *The Orchards Poetry Journal,* December 2016

"Cento Pantoum # 2" *119 Howl,* January 15, 2017

"The Cure for Everything." Silver Birch Press Blog, 2016

Thanks

I'd like to thank Professor Barbara L. Ungar, Professor Nancy White, Professor Greg Pardlo, and Professor Megan Fulwiler, all of whom I was privileged to study and write with. Additionally, a huge thank you to Sue, who has been a steady source of strength for me, for over twenty-five years. Finally, I thank my wife, Becky, and my daughter, Lily, for their unfailing support and tremendous love.

"For my family."

~ Carol H. Jewell

Nancy Wants Me to Go Deeper

Dig for the deeper stuff, she says,
write what you cannot say.
In the depths of the earth
diamonds are found.

Write what you cannot say
throw the dirt behind you in a frenzy for
diamonds which are found
past what you think your limits are.

The dirt falls in pieces behind me
I reach water; keep going
past what I think my limits are
rage my voice, and mean it.

I reach water: keep crying
through all the insults.
Find my rage and shout it—
Mother's dead; she can't reply.

Through all the pain
into the depths of the earth, me.
Mother's dead, no reply, still
Nancy wants me to go deeper.

Chestnuts, 1967

It's Saturday. Daddy and I
take the subway
into the city.
To the Museum of Natural History or
the Hayden Planetarium, or both, if there's time.
With Daddy's warm hand in mine, I feel safe.
Daddy knows all about the subway,
which trains to take, where to transfer.
He carries *The New York Times*, folded, under one arm.
The subway car rocks back and forth,
lulling some passengers to sleep.
Daddy reads his paper; I watch New York go by.
We get off the train and go upstairs.
The street
is noisy, the buildings and sky are gray.
We visit the Blue Whale.
We go to the Planetarium.
Later, I hold Daddy's hand again, and
we smell them, sweet smoky and hot:
chestnuts, roasting on a vendor's cart.
Daddy buys a bagful, we sit on a bench and eat them.
We take the subway back home; the chestnuts are gone.

Tribute

Watching films in class,
the old projector sputters
and flickers; the filmstrip catches
and melts, the sound wavers; we sleep.

The old projector sputters
to life. No one is drinking.
It melts and puts us to sleep.
and only the good kids take notes.

To life! Though no one is drinking,
we'll remember these times as great.
Only the good kids take notes,
Only they will write reports.

We remember these as great times
for which nothing can substitute.
Only the good kids will write reports;
I can't recall if that was me.

There was no substitute
for the flickering filmstrips.
I can't recall if I was good,
watching films in class.

The Embrace

The day finally over, I lie in quiet languor.
The old hammock, strung between two oaks
accepts my weary body, cradles me.
I close my eyes.

The sweet old hammock and the oaks
once forced-friends, now complementary.
I close my eyes against the noisy world,
a numinous breeze clears my head.

Once forced-friends, they now complement each other
The trees hold the hammock   hammock holds the trees, me.
The breeze, from heaven, relaxes body and mind.
But still, the heat, the heat of summer lingers.

Who holds whom? Oaks or hammock or me?
I ignore the din of daylight; I wait for sunset.
The heat of summer lengthens the day,
resilient.

I ignore the din of daylight, crave the coming evening.
My weary body gives in.
The resilient heat takes control of
the day finally over. I lie in quiet languor.

Cadence

I.   Agate palette,
      Queen Anne's Lace.

II.   Leaves pumpkin and rust,
      apple-cinnamon and gray skies.

III. Harry Lauder's Walking Stick,
      cardinal on snowy branch.

IV.   Mud season gives way,
      honeydew, viridian.

V.   Sudden storm, refreshing:
      the inviting hammock.

Literary Devices

Another purpose of enjambment is to continue
a rhythm that is stronger than a permanent end-stopping
wherein complicated
ideas are expressed in multiple lines.

Emily Dickinson in
   "With blue, uncertain, stumbling buzz,"
uses synesthesia----
while I, in this poem
   use inversion, and, while rhyming, do
not finish this thought---

But the most effective use of aposiopesis is seen when

Cento Pantoum #1

*(Sylvia Plath, Mary Oliver, Dylan Thomas, C.S. Lewis, John Keats,
Wallace Stevens, Walt Whitman, Richard Wilbur,
Harry Scott-Holland)*

I took a deep breath and listened to the old bray of my heart: I
am, I am, I am.
Listen, are you breathing just a little and calling it a life?
What can we do but keep on breathing in and out, modest and
willing, and in our places?
Rage, rage against the dying of the light.

Listen, are you breathing just a little and calling it a life?
Beauty is truth, truth beauty—
Rage, rage against the dying of the light.
Drink the whole summer down into the breast.

Beauty is truth, truth beauty—
Smeared with the gold of the opulent sun
Drink the whole summer down into the breast.
The morning air is all awash with angels.

Smeared with the gold of the opulent sun,
I sing the body electric.
The morning air is all awash with angels;
Life means all that it ever meant.

I sing the body electric!
What can we do but keep on breathing in and out, modest and
willing, and in our places?
Life means all that it ever meant.
I took a deep breath and listened to the old bray of my heart: I
am, I am, I am.

Cento Pantoum #2

*(Carolyn Kizer, Marilyn Hacker, Rachel Barenblat, Cecilia Woloch,
Louis MacNeice, John Ashbery, Nellie Wong, Mabel Ferrett,
Sean Edgley)*

Don't they know that we're supposed to be the stars?
I am the woman who makes up words
to keep the fire burning
of the wild, bright world.

I am the woman who makes up words,
felt with a phantom hunger
of the wild, bright world,
eyes shining without mystery.

Felt with a phantom hunger;
now, silently as one mounts a stair we emerge into the open,
eyes shining without mystery,
Gold bracelets, opal rings.

Now, silently as one mounts a stair we emerge into the open,
all lovely things undone:
gold bracelets, opal rings
unconscious of living.

All lovely things undone
to keep the fire burning,
unconscious of living.
Don't they know that we're supposed to be the stars?

Thanks

Thanks to the person
who put gas in the ambulance,
to the trainers who trained the volunteers.

Thanks for the decision
to be just downstairs, demonstrating CPR.
Thanks to the man who took control of the situation.

In my mind, I was back in Meriden
wrapped in the wild colors of my grandson's toys
scattered throughout the living room,
my daughter endlessly employed gathering them,
so she didn't know until
Tuesday night.

Thanks to the many people who didn't do anything stupid
to take the doctors' attention away when I needed it so badly.

Thanks to my brain for focus,
for tuning out all distractions to
concentrate on what the EMTs
instructions were. Thanks to the people who cleared
the pathways to the waiting
ambulance.

Thanks to the driver who
provided a smooth ride, despite
Albany's potholes.

Thanks to my sense of humor,
laughter and not sobs.

Thanks to the Five Quad volunteer
whose birthday I share; happy birthday to us!

Thanks to the love and concern of
strangers
all brought to me by God;
thanks to God for coming
to me that way.
Things look different

now.

Thanks to whomever
for opportunity. Like Yusef, I'm still
falling through its open silence.
Thanks for the
most delicious vanilla shake
I've ever had.

Thanks to the volunteers
who didn't hit their "snooze" button,
but showered and dressed and showed up,
who helped give me more days
to start anew,
to start everything anew.

Flashing

There are only so many layers a woman can remove.
I am in bed feeling fully clothed,
insulated as a hibernating bear.
Naked.
I wonder if I can shed my skin.

I awaken, clammy, in the unending night.
Rivulets of my age stream down me, puddle on the sheet.
My neighbor is running his lawn sprinkler.
I sneak downstairs—the cats look at me in drowsy wonder—
out of the house,
and run through the waterspray like a girl.

The Lines (after Adrienne Rich)

Try
pulsations into images
images into words.
illuminate, trust,
free yourself.
don't borrow:
steal.
a bird makes a nest
because she has to.
write because
no surprise
but the turn.

The Boxes of Your Stuff

still sitting in the garage.
I should have returned the library books
years ago.
I put them aside
thinking I would go through them
later.

They say Crane Mountain now has
over 200 climbing trails.
I know I'll never go back.
Winter is coming, I know.
I think of the mountain in the snow.
I trace your name in the air, where you are.

The Dream

I dreamed you alive,
all the good parts of you still good,
all your sorrows fleeting,
whole and well-formed, on fire!

All the good parts of you still good,
climbing the mountain with me:
whole and well-formed, on fire,
muscular, full of breath, and smiling.

You climbed the mountain with me.
Told me jokes, and sang,
muscular, full of breath, and smiling.
I hoped never to awaken.

With laughs and song,
all you never were; I long for that now.
I hoped never to awaken.
In June I scattered your ashes into the wind.

All you never were, that I long for now,
all your sorrows fleeting…
I scattered your ashes into the wind, yet
I dreamed you alive.

22

Early Fall into Winter, Northeastern New York

Fields of Giant Purple Hyssop
b o r d e r the road. Not to be outdone,
Joe Pye Weed e d g e s the creek.
Cardinal Flowers join their feathered
cousins, and I would have seen more
of them if my neighbor hadn't mown
my wildflower meadow down.

Autumn looks brighter against a gray sky
than a blue one.
Your voice sounded
more vibrant in a smoky bar
than in a quiet room.

Fall progresses into red, gold, and brown,
and only the pines remain
green as my memory of you
fades to gray.
When the snow falls here in the valley,
heavy and brisk,
I think of you up at Crane Mountain Pond:
no eyes to see with, no heart to grasp.

Brother-Memory

Why do I think of you in springtime?
Rivulets of frosted mountain
water rushing down
toward town.

In summer?
You'd spend
endless days
in boyhood bliss, even
as a man.

Autumn?
We'd jump in piles of leaves fallen to the crisp ground—

Silent pallor, snow
drifts.
But my mug is warm,
and, somewhere, you are
sledding down a never-ending hill.

Attachment

Doctor says, *Not a good week? How can I help you?*
Closes the door to her quiet office.
You can help me by not leaving, you answer,
settling into the leather couch across from her.
Even though you know it's impossible --she's leaving--
even though she agrees with you --she's leaving--

You can help me by not leaving, you answer again,
as you settle into the buttery couch.
You say it's not enough; you want more.
She agrees with you, but she's leaving.
She asks *What would "more" look like?*

It's never enough, you always want more:
from her voice on the phone to the scarce,
historic email, the annual paperwhites.
She repeats, *What would "more" look like?*
You weep; she knows what you want.

From her voice on the phone to the scarce historic email,
the annual paperwhites.
It's warm, her voice, and you can read between the lines.
You weep; she knows what you want.
Why is she making you beg?

It's warm, her voice, and I can read between her lines
Even though I know it's impossible --she's leaving.
Why is she making me beg?
She asks again, *how can I help?* Her office, a quiet refrain.

Furtive

I read your poems
in secret places: my desk,
my bed, under the covers.
I want to touch them, you.
Your key fits my lock: we
connect, one-sidedly, and
only I am aware.
I close my desk to hide
treasures old and tucked inside
my mind, away from you,
but with you.
Time to turn inward, indeed,
to find oneself
under the fallen leaves.
Again, I wash down the autumnal blood
from my wounded memory.

Some People Say

Some people say
that you two should
never have had;
that you were
probably made;
that you met
only some of;
that both of
you were;
that both
were looking;
that both of you
were lonely alone;
that neither of you
knew how;
that you two should
never have had children;
some people say.

Carolina '81

Remember the red brick so slippery in the rain?
Such a confusing time and school on top of it all.
We were so, so young,
a friendship lost and found.

We were so confused and had school on top of it all.
I remember you outside the ice cream shop,
a friendship lost and found.
If you wait long enough, you meet everyone.

I remember you outside the ice cream shop;
"What are YOU doing here?"
If you wait long enough, you meet everyone,
but you can find out you aren't who you think.

"What are YOU doing here?"
What is a friend; what is love?
You can find out you aren't who you think.
They say hindsight is 20/20.

What is a friend; what is love?
We were so, so young.
They say hindsight is 20/20.
Remember the red brick so slippery in the rain?

Crestfallen

You said you didn't remember my little notes,
the ones that said *I love you* in so many different ways.
I said I recalled yours, the ones you left in my office;
they meant and mean so much to me.

Different ways to say *I love you*
in various languages, or in favorite meals,
that meant and mean so much,
like a touch, a hug, being together

in various tongues and flavors.
How do you feel loved?
A touch, a hug, together
sharing books, making music.

How do I feel loved?
Memories link to scent, but
books and music work well, too.
How will I sit in your memories?

Scents fixed to memories…
I said I recalled your notes to me, in my office.
How will I sit in your memories?
You didn't remember the notes I left you.

My Fears

I.

I've always said
I didn't care what happened to me
after I was dead
as long as I was
really dead.
Please don't bury me
alive.

II.

I've always said
I didn't care what happened to me
I'm not afraid of death
I'm afraid of pain.

III.

I've always said
I didn't care what happened to me
after I died, as long as
I died first.

IV.

Please don't die first.

Ode to Provincetown

From Commercial Street, I can see
the Pilgrim Monument, topped by its
"Donald Duck" visage,
seagoing boats,
tourists looking for whales,
an unnamed beach at low tide
with a cantering horse and rider, bareback,
the public library--built in 1860,
competing stands of salt water taffy,
pretty boys, bears, and fairies,
snowqueens, dykes, and femmes,
tweeners and giddy teens,
posters: GET TESTED. BE SAFE. NO SMOKING,

your green eyes, smiling at me

If you want to write a love poem

you must include:
>the night we fell asleep inside each other,
>velvet and warm,
>pink petals spread across pillows,
>you feeding me briny olives, one by one,
>a vanilla-scented candle,
>fuchsite eyes,
>Chrissie Hynde on the small stereo,
>"The Lottery" by Shirley Jackson,
>your downy skin,
>finally reaching the itch in the small of my back.

The Cure for Everything

I know the cure for everything: Salt water...in one form or another: Sweat, tears or the sea.– *The Deluge at Norderney, Seven Gothic Tales*, 1934 (Karen Blixen/Isak Dinesen)

I.

Back
        b
         r
          e
           a
            k
              i
                n
                  g
pulling or pushing
to get
something out
bandana on your head
or
sunhat, dripping
your face
your eyes
the summer garden
the labor bed.

II.

How long do I cry for
all
of
you
how many shirtfronts
are drenched
red eyes RED EYES
hair mussed
snot smeared
a sting, a long ache:
the unending bellow.
III.

I know you dislike
sand between your toes

most fish, shellfish
I put on my w i d e
brimmed hat
take your hand
walk in the low tide
until it's time to go;
the sunset.

Carol H. Jewell

Carol H. Jewell is a musician, teacher, librarian, and poet living in Upstate New York with her wife and eight cats. She received her MFA in Creative Writing from The College of Saint Rose in 2016.

CPSIA information can be obtained
at www.ICGtesting.com
Printed in the USA
BVHW051253030423
661653BV00009B/324

9 781947 653108